PERCUSSION

MOVIE FAVORITES

Solos and Band Arrangements
Correlated with Essential Elements Band Method

Arranged by
MICHAEL SWEENEY

Welcome to Essential Elements Movie Favorites! This Percussion book includes parts for both Percussion 1 and Percussion 2 of the full band arrangements. A SOLO version of these selections may be found in the Keyboard Percussion book. Optional accompaniment recordings are available separately in CD or cassette format. Use these recordings when playing solos for friends and family.

ISBN 978-0-7935-5956-5

HAL•LEONARD
CORPORATION
7777 W. BLUEMOUND RD. P.O. BOX 13819 MILWAUKEE, WI 53213

00860012

From The Universal Motion Picture JURASSIC PARK

Theme From "JURASSIC PARK"

PERCUSSION 1
Band Arrangement

Composed by JOHN WILLIAMS
Arranged by MICHAEL SWEENEY

Calmly

MCA music publishing

Theme From "JURASSIC PARK"

PERCUSSION 2
Band Arrangement

Composed by JOHN WILLIAMS
Arranged by MICHAEL SWEENEY

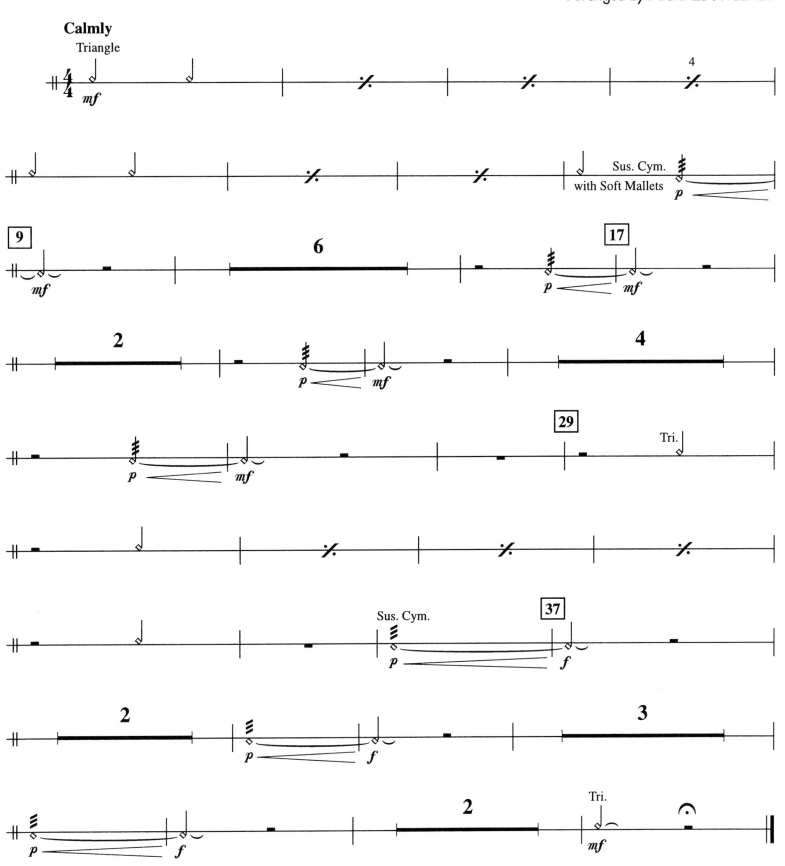

MCA music publishing

From CHARIOTS OF FIRE
CHARIOTS OF FIRE

Music by VANGELIS
Arranged by MICHAEL SWEENEY

PERCUSSION 1
Band Arrangement

Moderately

*Play with brushes
throughout if possible

00860012

CHARIOTS OF FIRE

PERCUSSION 2
Band Arrangement

Music by VANGELIS
Arranged by MICHAEL SWEENEY

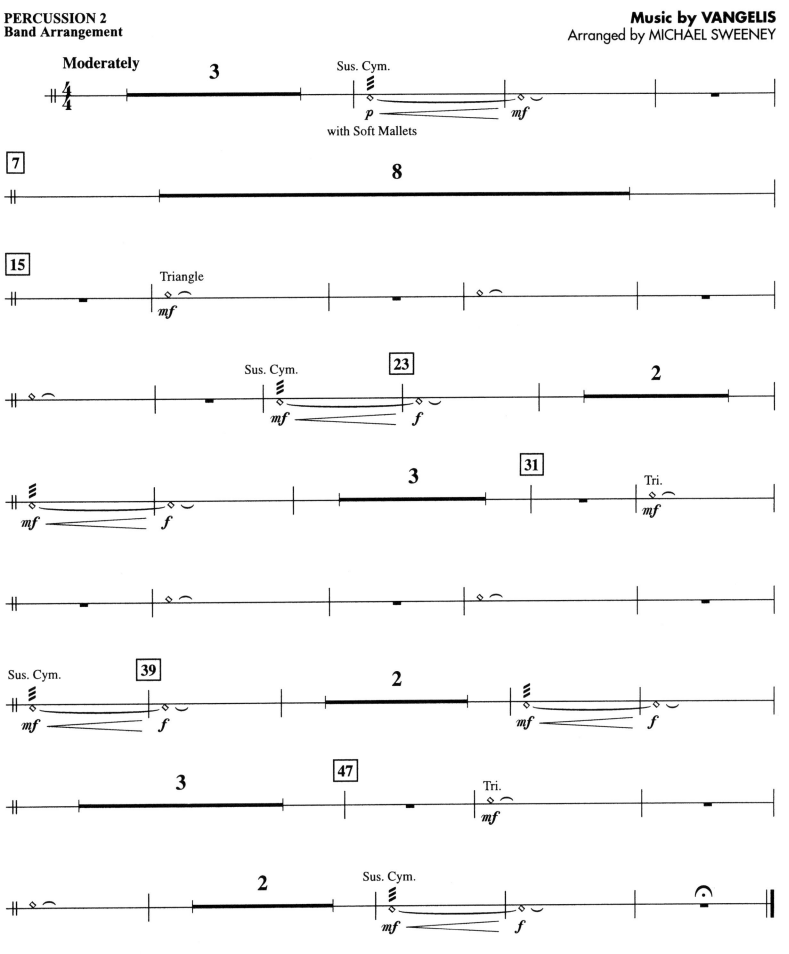

From THE MAN FROM SNOWY RIVER

THE MAN FROM SNOWY RIVER
(Main Title Theme)

PERCUSSION 1
Band Arrangement

By BRUCE ROWLAND
Arranged by MICHAEL SWEENEY

From THE MAN FROM SNOWY RIVER

THE MAN FROM SNOWY RIVER
(Main Title Theme)

PERCUSSION 2
Band Arrangement

By BRUCE ROWLAND
Arranged by MICHAEL SWEENEY

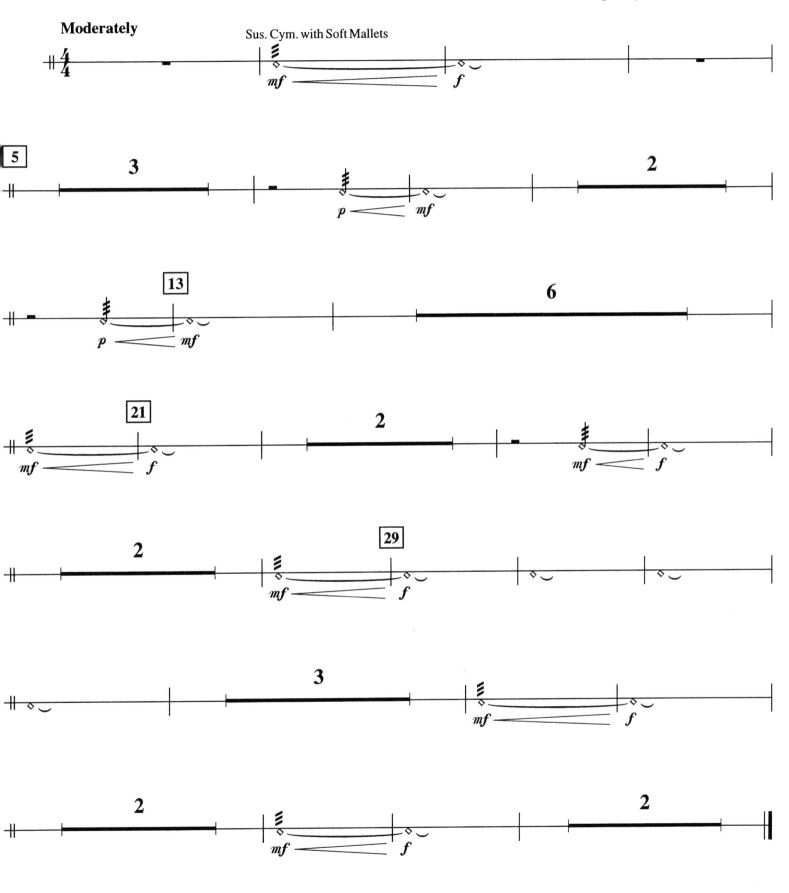

From The Paramount Motion Picture FORREST GUMP

FORREST GUMP - MAIN TITLE

(Feather Theme)

PERCUSSION 1
Band Arrangement

Music by ALAN SILVESTRI
Arranged by MICHAEL SWEENEY

*Hold stick in left hand. Strike rim of drum with butt end of stick while keeping the tip on the center of the head.

From The Paramount Motion Picture FORREST GUMP

FORREST GUMP - MAIN TITLE

(Feather Theme)

PERCUSSION 2
Band Arrangement

Music by ALAN SILVESTRI
Arranged by MICHAEL SWEENEY

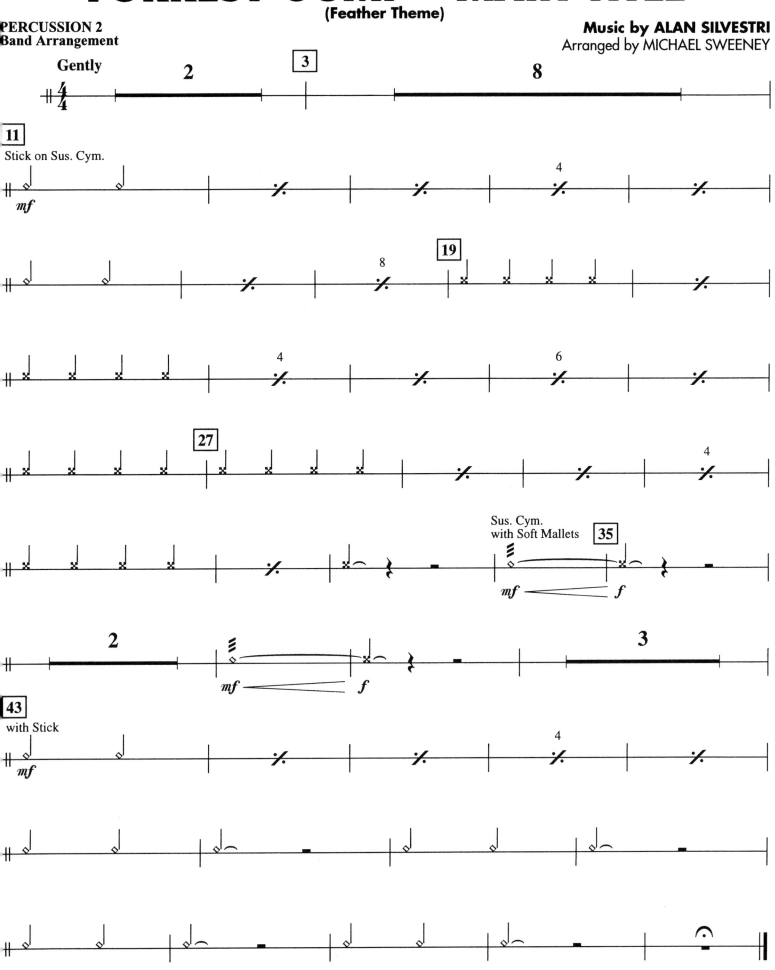

0860012

From AN AMERICAN TAIL

SOMEWHERE OUT THERE

Words and Music by JAMES HORNER,
BARRY MANN and CYNTHIA WEIL
Arranged by MICHAEL SWEENEY

PERCUSSION 1
Band Arrangement

MCA music publishing

From AN AMERICAN TAIL

SOMEWHERE OUT THERE

Words and Music by JAMES HORNER,
BARRY MANN and CYNTHIA WEIL

Arranged by MICHAEL SWEENEY

PERCUSSION 2
Band Arrangement

Moderately Slow

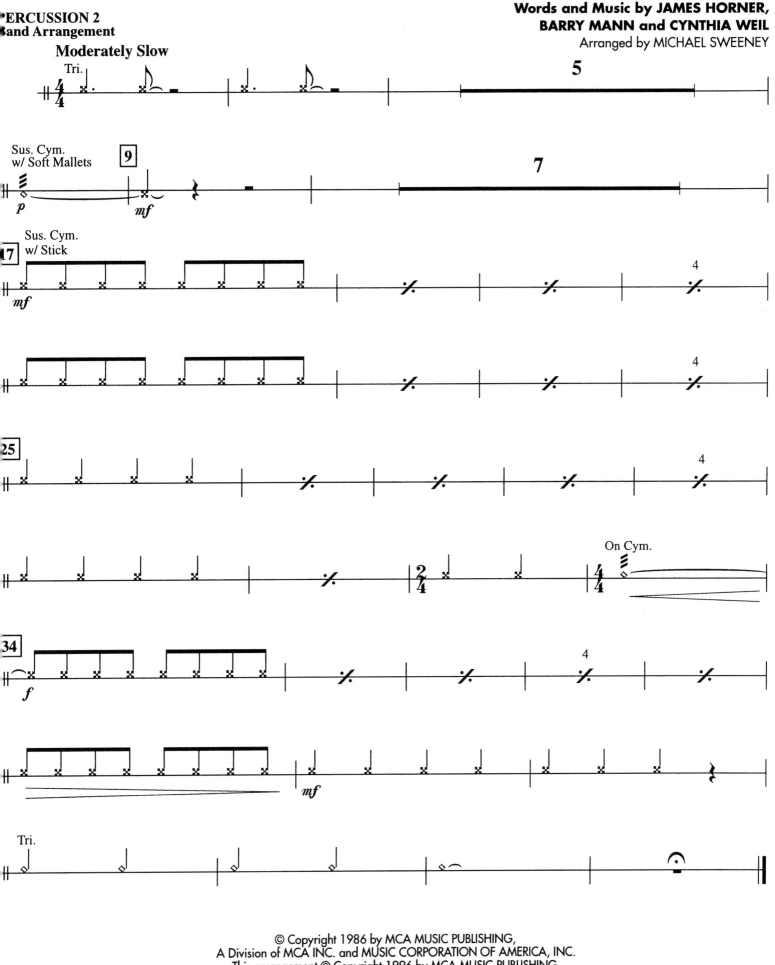

MCA music publishing

0860012

From DANCES WITH WOLVES
THE JOHN DUNBAR THEME

PERCUSSION 1
Band Arrangement

By JOHN BARRY
Arranged by MICHAEL SWEENEY

From **DANCES WITH WOLVES**
THE JOHN DUNBAR THEME

PERCUSSION 2
Band Arrangement

By JOHN BARRY
Arranged by MICHAEL SWEENEY

00860012

From The Paramount Motion Picture RAIDERS OF THE LOST ARK

RAIDERS MARCH

By JOHN WILLIAMS
Arranged by MICHAEL SWEENEY

PERCUSSION 1
Band Arrangement

00860012

RAIDERS MARCH

PERCUSSION 2
Band Arrangement

By JOHN WILLIAMS
Arranged by MICHAEL SWEENEY

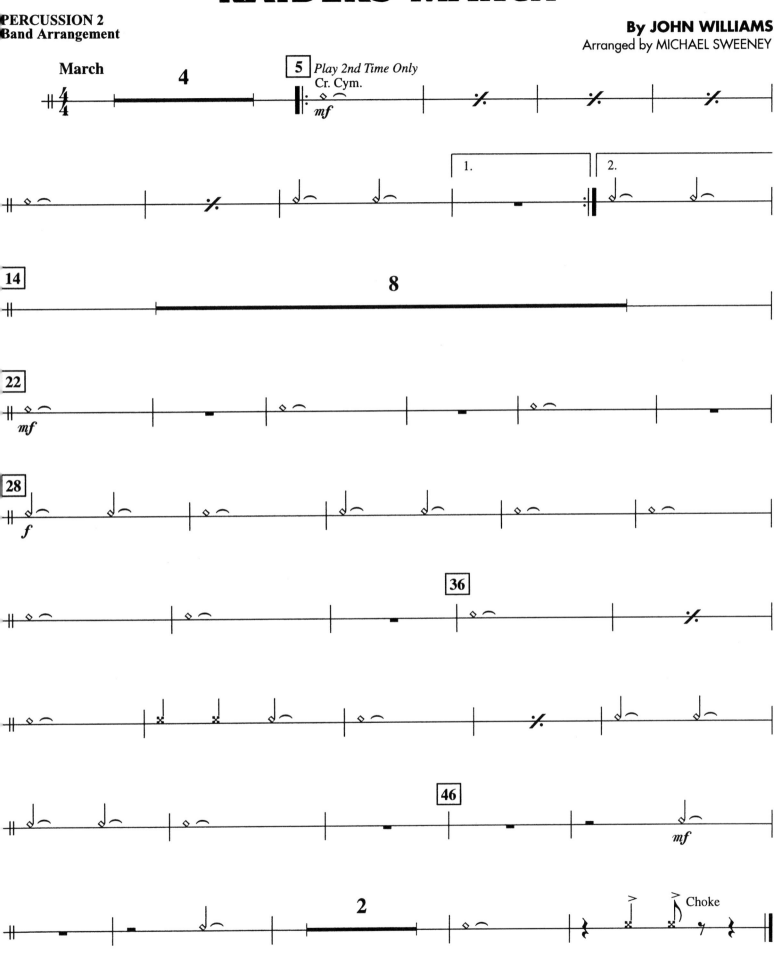

00860012

From APOLLO 13
APOLLO 13
(End Credits)

By JAMES HORNER
Arranged by MICHAEL SWEENEY

PERCUSSION 1
Band Arrangement

MCA music publishing

From APOLLO 13
APOLLO 13
(End Credits)

PERCUSSION 2
Band Arrangement

By JAMES HORNER
Arranged by MICHAEL SWEENEY

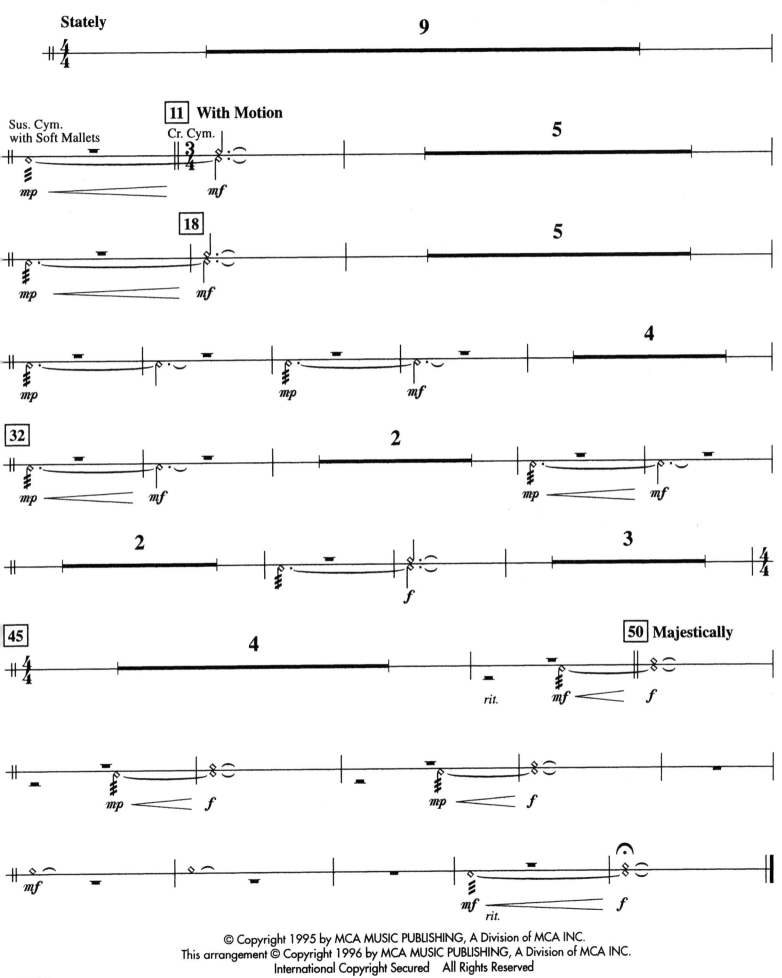

MCA music publishing

From The Universal Picture E.T. (THE EXTRA-TERRESTRIAL)

THEME FROM E.T. (THE EXTRA-TERRESTRIAL)

PERCUSSION 1
Band Arrangement

Music by JOHN WILLIAMS
Arranged by MICHAEL SWEENEY

MCA music publishing

THEME FROM E.T. (THE EXTRA-TERRESTRIAL)

PERCUSSION 2
Band Arrangement

Music by JOHN WILLIAMS
Arranged by MICHAEL SWEENEY

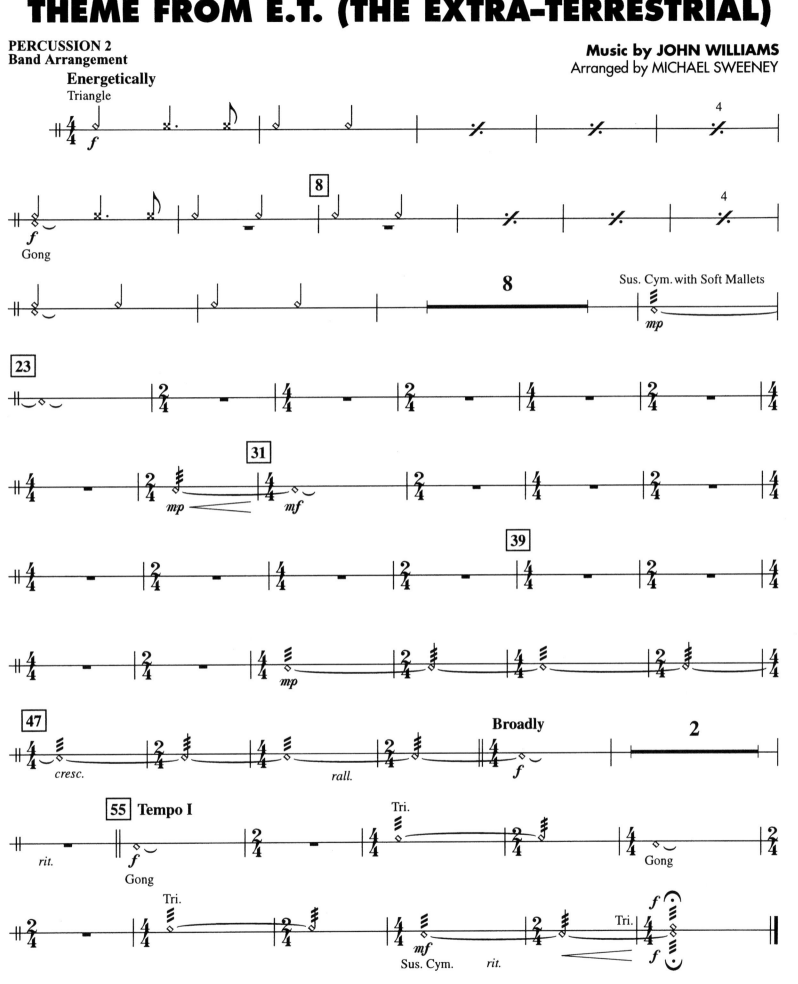

MCA music publishing

Theme From The Paramount Picture STAR TREK

STAR TREK®-THE MOTION PICTURE

PERCUSSION 1
Band Arrangement

Music by JERRY GOLDSMITH
Arranged by MICHAEL SWEENEY

00860012

STAR TREK®-THE MOTION PICTURE

PERCUSSION 2
Band Arrangement

Music by JERRY GOLDSMITH
Arranged by MICHAEL SWEENEY

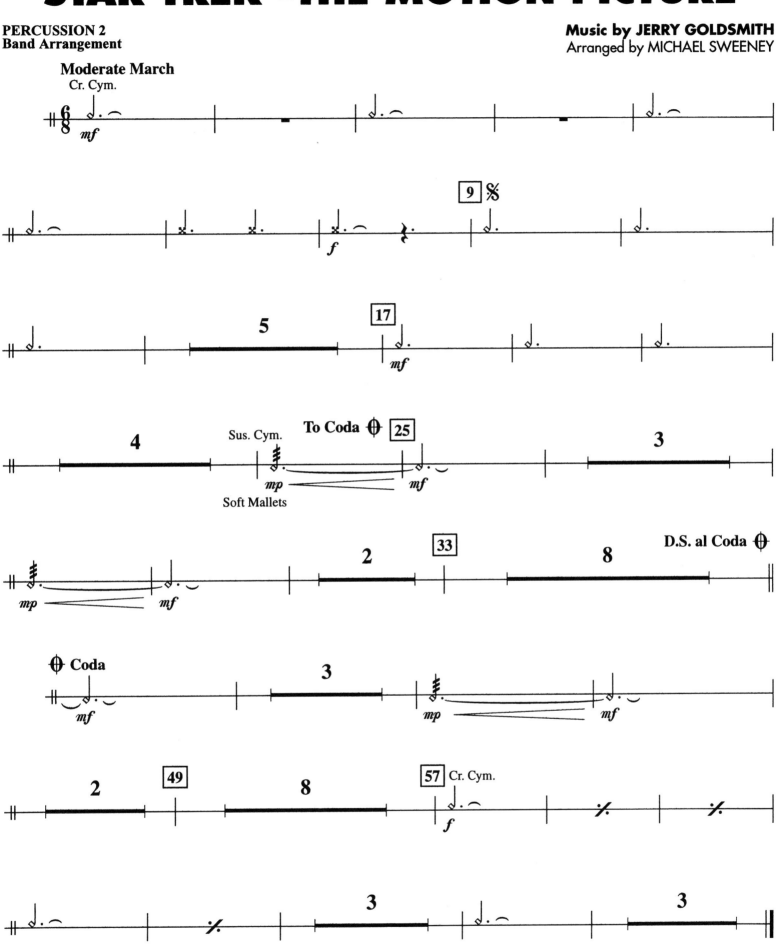

00860012

From The Universal Motion Picture BACK TO THE FUTURE

BACK TO THE FUTURE

PERCUSSION 1
Band Arrangement

By ALAN SILVESTRI
Arranged by MICHAEL SWEENEY

MCA music publishing

00860012

BACK TO THE FUTURE

From The Universal Motion Picture BACK TO THE FUTURE

PERCUSSION 2
Band Arrangement

By ALAN SILVESTRI
Arranged by MICHAEL SWEENEY

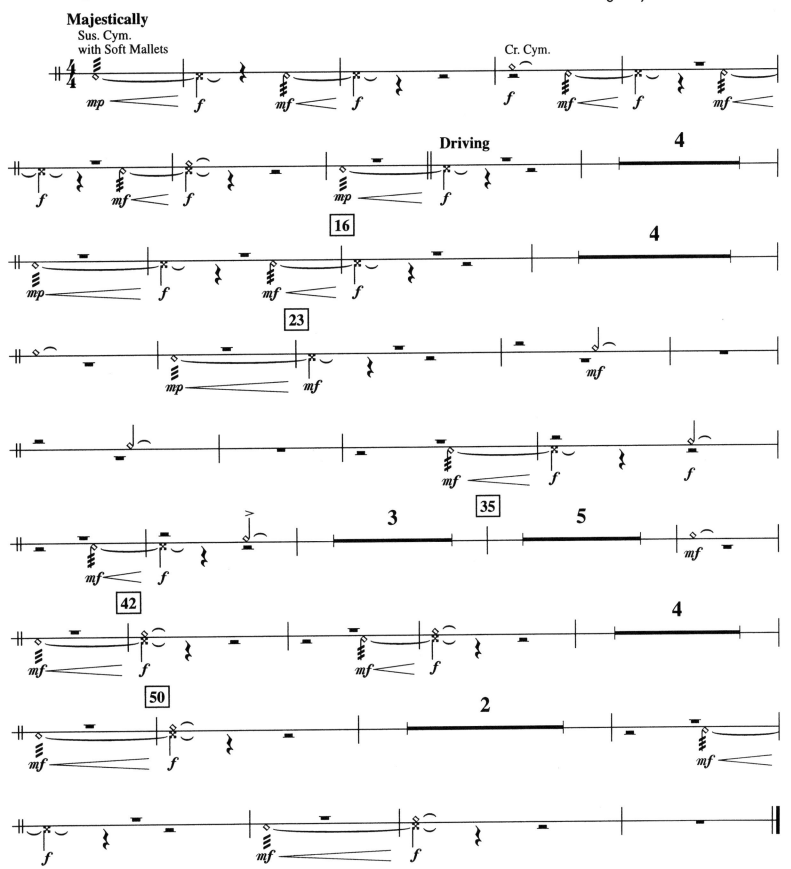

MCA music publishing